Collectible Meals

Collectible Meals

Real Menus from History and Hollywood

by Rob DiSilvestre

Unlimited Publishing
Bloomington, Indiana

Copyright © 2002 by Rob DiSilvestre

Distributing Publisher:
Unlimited Publishing LLC
Bloomington, Indiana

http://www.unlimitedpublishing.com

Contributing Publisher:
Rob DiSilvestre

Cover and book design by Charles King. Copyright © 2002 by Unlimited Publishing LLC. This book was typeset with Adobe® InDesign®, using the Adobe Garamond®, Myriad®, and Adobe Jensen® typefaces. This book makes use of one or more typefaces specifically licensed by and customized for the exclusive use of Unlimited Publishing LLC.

All rights reserved under Title 17, U.S. Code, International and Pan-American Copyright Conventions. No part of this work may be reproduced or transmitted in any form or by any means, electronic or mechanical, including photocopying, scanning, recording or duplication by any information storage or retrieval system without prior written permission from the author(s) and publisher(s), except for the inclusion of brief quotations with attribution in a review or report. Requests for reproductions or related information should be addressed to the author(s) c/o Unlimited Publishing LLC. See www.unlimitedpublishing.com for mailing address.

Unlimited Publishing LLC provides worldwide book design, printing, marketing and distribution services for professional writers and small to mid-size presses, serving as distributing publisher. Sole responsibility for the content of each work rests with the author(s) and/or contributing publisher(s). The opinions expressed herein may not be interpreted in any way as representing those of Unlimited Publishing, nor any of its affiliates.

First Edition

Copies of this book and others
are available to order online at:

http://www.unlimitedpublishing.com/authors

ISBN 1-58832-073-1 HARDBACK
ISBN 1-58832-071-5 PAPERBACK

Unlimited Publishing
Bloomington, Indiana

Acknowledgments

The day after a spectacular gourmet meal at our new neighbor's home, my wife and I wondered how we could possibly offer anything as enjoyable in return. I recalled an anecdote about a meal that Katherine Hepburn prepared for her longtime lover Spencer Tracy. After some research, I found the story and noted the menu. We served that meal to our new friends the following weekend and spent a delightful evening dining and discussing the genesis of our menu. *Collectible Meals* was born that night. (The Hepburn-Tracy meal can be found in this book.)

Special thanks, then, to Danielle Baril for her inspiring culinary skill and to Ron Crebo, for his enthusiastic and consistent support throughout this project. They have truly been involved in *Collectible Meals* from the very beginning.

Thanks also to the thousands of people who have visited at www.CollectibleMeals.com. Our collection of menus continues to grow and interest in this hobby continues to increase.

The "writing the book" part would have never happened without the technical and artistic expertise of many people and I don't want to leave anyone out, so I'll simply say thanks so much to all for your help. Anyone who takes on the task of editing my work is at the very least courageous; Scott Kearns is that and extremely talented as well. From Hilton Head to Harper's Ferry to Homosassa, my family has never wavered in supporting me. My children, Katie and Robby, remain my inspiration.

Finally, while I wrote the words and did the research—any mistakes are mine—my wife Ann truly made this book possible. I wish my writing was good enough to explain how much that means to me.

— Rob DiSilvestre

List of Menus

(in mostly alphabetical order)

First Academy Awards Banquet • 1
Achilles & Odysseus • 3
John and Abigail Adams • 5
Humphrey Bogart & Lauren Bacall • 7
Ted Bundy • 9
George Burns & Friend • 11
George Bush and Bill Clinton… • 13
…and George W. Bush • 15
Jimmy Carter • 17
Fidel Castro… • 20
… and John F. Kennedy Jr. • 21
Patsy Cline • 24
Jane Fonda & Ted Turner • 26
Gary Gilmore • 27
Ulysses S. Grant • 29
Sammy "The Bull" Gravano • 32
Katherine Hepburn & Spencer Tracy • 34
Thomas Jefferson • 36
Grace Kelly • 39
John F. Kennedy… • 41
… and P. J. Nehru • 44
Robert E. Lee • 46
Abraham Lincoln • 48
Marilyn Monroe • 51
Richard Nixon • 53
Elvis Presley… • 56
… and Natalie Wood • 57
… and The Beatles • 58
Ronald Reagan… • 60

… and Queen Elizabeth • 62
…and Presidents Nixon, Ford, Carter and Bush • 64
Franklin Delano Roosevelt • 66
Paul Simon • 68
Frank Sinatra • 69
Princess Diana • 71
Jimmy Stewart • 74
Elizabeth Taylor & Richard Burton • 75
Astronaut Andrew Thomas • 78
The Titanic • 80
Karla Faye Tucker • 82
Gianni Versace • 83
George Washington • 85
John Wayne • 89
Mae West • 91
Duke and Duchess of Windsor • 93
Tiger Woods • 95

In the next Collectible Meals.... • 97

Introduction

MOST OF US AT ONE TIME OR ANOTHER have invited a neighbor over for a backyard cookout. A typical menu of tossed salad, grilled steak and ice cream dessert makes a pleasant but rarely memorable meal.

What if you knew that precise menu was the same one Katherine Hepburn served to Spencer Tracy after a day of filming the movie classic *Inherit the Wind*?

Suddenly, your ordinary cookout is an event, sparking a conversation about Hepburn and Tracy, the movie, or maybe Hollywood in general. Your routine meal shows a spark of creativity and originality; the menu has become an active catalyst to your party.

Welcome to the world of *Collectible Meals*.

Menus in this collection include Robert E. Lee on the battlefield, the last meal of mass murderer Ted Bundy, Marilyn Monroe after posing for her famous nude calendar photo, and President Nixon in the White House as he prepared to resign.

Collectibles are tangible pieces of history. The night before he was assassinated, President John F. Kennedy stayed in the Rice Hotel in Texas. He left behind some unsigned doodles on Rice Hotel stationery. Those doodles recently sold at auction for $11,500. For breakfast the following morning, JFK had a soft-boiled egg breakfast. For less than a dollar, you can recreate his entire meal; it is a fun, accessible way to share an historic moment. It is inexpensive, authentic, verifiable and available to everyone.

The "rules" of *Collectible Meals* are simple: find the menu of a meal shared by a celebrity/historical figure and the circumstances surrounding that meal. Knowing the main dish only (usually) doesn't count. Document the time and place of the meal. Tell the story, replicate the menu and—presto—your ordinary meal is transformed into an entertaining, historic re-enactment.

Serve the romantic breakfast shared by Princess Diana and Dodi al Fayed on their tragic last morning together.

How about a spooky "last meal" this Halloween, the same one ordered by murderer Gary Gilmore prior to his execution?

Have a Christmas brunch enjoyed by George and Martha Washington way back in 1769.

Lunch with Grace Kelly, dinner with Cary Grant.

Collectible Meals can transform a routine meal into a history lesson or celebration. There is a collectible meal fit for every occasion. Recreate the midnight supper Elvis Presley served to the Beatles. Serve the banquet menu at the first Academy Awards while you watch this year's awards. From elaborate holiday feasts to simple lunches between friends, there is a meal fit for every occasion, every skill level and every budget.

The following pages contain meals from Humphrey Bogart to Tiger Woods. The menu of these meals—not the ingredients—will separate your collectible dish from an ordinary serving. This is not a book of recipes.

How you prepare the meal doesn't really matter. There is the occasional suggestion of a recipe (see Lauren Bacall's instructions for preparing a proper martini) or a recommendation on an appropriate substitute for food that is out of favor in today's kitchen (see *terrapin soup* in the Academy Awards and John Adams meals). Otherwise, let your skill in the kitchen dictate your recipe and allow your storytelling ability and imagination to make your meal a success. From the glamour of Hollywood to the echoes of heroes and hoodlums throughout history, turn your dining table into an exploration of some special people and special times in our past.

— ✦ —

First Academy Awards Banquet

On May 16, 1929, The Academy of Motion Picture Arts and Sciences held its first Academy Awards banquet. Among the winners:

> Best Picture—Paramount Pictures' *Wings*
> Best Actress—Janet Gaynor
> Best Actor—Emil Jannings

The event was held in the Blossom Room of the Roosevelt Hotel in Hollywood. Approximately 250 people attended; tickets cost just $10. Unlike today, the winners were known well in advance, so suspense played no role in the ceremonies. Nevertheless, this was an opportunity to promote the motion picture industry and celebrate with friends and colleagues. It was the first of fifteen consecutive banquets and the only ceremony not on radio or television. The popularity of the event doomed the banquets and forced the change to today's more familiar theater-style presentation.

On the menu that first night:

Terrapin Soup

Jumbo Squab Perigeaux

Lobster Eugenia

L.A. Salad

Fruit Supreme

In addition to the "Best" awards, two special awards were given—to Warner Brothers for producing the groundbreaking talking picture, *The Jazz Singer*; and to Charlie Chaplin for producing, directing, writing and starring in *The Circus*.

Al Jolson's first words in *The Jazz Singer* would prove prophetic for both the industry and the Academy Awards ceremony: "You ain't seen nothin' yet!"

Author's Note: You will find several other meals in these pages which also call for some version of terrapin (or turtle) soup, which for many years was a common and popular dish. It is rarely available today. Any beef-stock based vegetable soup with chicken added to it makes an effective substitute for terrapin soup. The chicken—or any mild fish—will offer a hint of turtle flavor when marinated in the beef stock.

Achilles & Odysseus

IN GREEK MYTHOLOGY, the Trojan War began when Paris of Troy abducted Helen, wife of the Greek king of Sparta. When the Trojans refused to return Helen, Agamemnon assembled an army led by many of the great Greek heroes. For the next nine years, these heroes surrounded and attacked Troy but were unsuccessful in taking the city. Finally, they resorted to deceit by constructing a huge wooden horse and concealing a small group of soldiers inside. As the rest of the army appeared to sail for home, the Greek warrior Sinon persuaded the Trojans to bring the wooden horse inside the city walls. That night, the army returned, the soldiers snuck out of the horse and opened the city gates; Troy was reduced to ruin.

Homer wrote that during the nine-year siege Achilles hosted a meal for Odysseus outside the walls of Ilium. Patroclus, son of King Menoetius and himself a Greek hero, prepared the legendary warriors' meal with help from Automedon.

On this 12th century B.C. menu:

Sheep's Back

Goat

Chine of a Wild Hog
(knitted, carved, salted and roasted on spits)

Baskets of Bread

Author's note: *Sheep's back, hog fat and goat meat are not often found in today's supermarkets. Bread in the twelfth century bears little resemblance to today's baked treats. With that in mind, the official Collectible Meals position is that it is OK to just tell this story and, in the spirit of the warriors' battlefield encampment, serve a barbecue or some type of shish-ka-bob from the grill.*

John and Abigail Adams

Photo courtesy Still Pictures Branch, National Archives

JOHN ADAMS had a long and distinguished career as one of the Founding Fathers of our nation. He was elected as the second President of the United States and was the first to live in the White House. He was a member of the committee assigned by the Continental Congress to write the Declaration of Independence and one of the signers of the Declaration.

Legend has this meal being served at the home of John and Abigail Adams on July 4, 1776. However, the Continental Congress had voted to approve the Declaration of Independence on July 2, 1776. Adams was one of the principal architects of the Declaration; he, like most members of the Congress, assumed that July 2 would be forever known as Independence Day. He wrote a letter to Abigail on July 4 describing the historic events of the week; he certainly could not have hand delivered it.

Abigail Adams did create this menu and served the meal as a holiday tradition, she most likely first served the meal following Adams' return from Europe after a stint as U.S. Ambassador. Wife Abigail recalled a meal she had served back in 1773; since the main dish and vegetables were fresh, seasonal and native to her beloved New England, she considered it to be uniquely American. She and her husband served this meal every year on the Fourth of July until President Adams' death, ironically on July 4, in 1826.

Her Fourth of July meal became a tradition not only in the second president's home, but also throughout New England. It was featured at the Festival of Gas Restaurant during the World's Fair in New York in 1964 and 1965.

On the menu:

— ❧ —

Green Turtle Soup
New England Salmon with Egg Sauce
New Potatoes
Early Peas
Apple Pan Dowdy

— ❧ —

Humphrey Bogart & Lauren Bacall

Humphrey Bogart and Lauren Bacall were one of Hollywood's most famous couples. Combined with their immense acting talents, their off-screen party exploits and romance/marriage made their pairing a true Hollywood legend.

Bogey starred in many of the most popular films of all time, including *Casablanca, The African Queen* and *The Maltese Falcon*. He also starred in *Treasure of the Sierra Madre, Sabrina* and *Key Largo* among many others. He was nominated three times for an Academy Award, winning the Best Actor for a Leading Role award for 1954's *The Caine Mutiny*.

In 1944, Bogart was already one of the most popular actors in the world and he lived the hard-charging movie star life. His yacht was the scene for many weekends of fishing, gambling and entertaining friends including close friends Spencer Tracy, John Wayne and director John Ford. Bogart was assigned the starring role in a movie called *To Have and Have Not* based on an Ernest Hemingway novel and directed by Howard Hawks. The female lead was given to 19-year-old "Betty" Bacall in her first starring role. Bacall's character was named "Slim", Bogey's was called "Harry", although Slim called him Steve in one of the most memorable lines in movie history: "You know how to whistle, don't you Steve? You just put your lips together and blow."

Bogey and Bacall fell in love during filming; they were married in 1945. Their son Steve was named after Bogey's character in that first memorable film pairing. Bogey and Bacall went on to appear in many other films together, although none were as memorable as *To Have and Have Not*. Bacall became a leading lady in her own right, starring in films for over fifty years, from 1953's *How to Marry a Millionaire* with Marilyn Monroe to 1976's *The Shootist* with John Wayne, to 1999's *Presence of Mind*.

Although their romance was a volatile one, it endured until Bogey's death in 1957. In fact, when asked late in his life about his happiest times, he was quoted as saying, "…when I was courting Betty."

The couple first lived in Villa #8 at the Garden of Allah in Los Angeles. During the second week of March 1944, they attended a small dinner party at Gloria and Arthur Sheekman's in the apartment complex. Sheekman's daughter Sylvia recalled the menu:

—— ❧ ——

Chicken Pot Pie

Guacamole with Tortilla Chips

Dry Martinis

—— ❧ ——

Sheekman remembered that Bacall liked her martinis *very* dry, saying, "Just pass the vermouth over the glass!"

Ted Bundy

Ted Bundy was a handsome, articulate man who had attended law school and publicly presented himself as a popular, successful, politically active member of his community. By the early 1970s, the long-time resident of the Northeast worked for the Republican Party and volunteered at a crisis clinic. In private, he spent much of his time abducting, raping and murdering young women.

His killing spree is believed to have begun in the Seattle area. He was first arrested and convicted of aggravated kidnapping in 1975. While still in jail, police continued to link Bundy to a series of horrific crimes; he was finally charged with murder in 1976. As he pretended to prepare for his own defense in that case, he escaped. Although recaptured, he again escaped. Bundy fled to Florida, where in 1978 he was arrested and charged for the multiple murders in the Chi Omega sorority house massacre on the Florida State campus. While in jail on those charges, he was charged with the murder of Kimberly Leach, a twelve-year-old girl from Lake City, Florida.

Bundy turned his trials into pure theater, acting as his own counsel and attempting a series of bizarre and ineffective legal maneuvers. He was convicted and sentenced to die in the Florida electric chair for young Kimberly's murder, as well as the Chi Omega murders. In an attempt to stay alive, Bundy offered a series of frantic appeals and a flurry of "deals" to provide details of other murders he had committed. Law enforcement finally lost their patience with him and his court appeals ran out on January 23, 1989.

Although he would not die until the next day, Bundy knew that his best efforts to keep himself alive were over. For his last meal, he chose a Mexican theme.

On the menu:

— ❧ —

Burritos
Mexican Rice
Salad

— ❧ —

Bundy terrified and fascinated the American public like no murderer since Charles Manson. He eventually confessed to twenty-eight murders, yet his handsome, articulate manner continued to attract far too many women even from his prison cell. Even today, his case continues to interest the public. His arrest, conviction and ultimate death has inspired numerous books, articles and movies.

George Burns & Friend

During the 1920's, George Burns was a young vaudeville star known as "Nat" Burns. He was dating the beautiful Gracie Allen. Along with his friend Archibald Leach, a mime and stilt walker from a touring acrobatic troupe, he used to go for dinner at the Automat in Times Square.

The New York vend shop was part of a popular chain of "waiterless restaurants" in the pre-fast food chain era. It was a popular hangout for actors, musicians and the cabaret crowd, especially late at night. The Automat was well known as a place for fresh, inexpensive food and automated service.

The most expensive item on the menu was fifteen cents. Even that was a steep price for a vaudeville actor. Burns would wait for someone else to pick up their order and use one of his sister's hairpins to jam the window and get his favorite meal at no charge.

On the menu:

Beef Stew

Burns' romance with Gracie Allen became one of Hollywood's greatest love stories. The death of vaudeville only breathed new life for the film and TV career of Burns, most notably in *The George Burns and Gracie Allen Comedy Hour* and movies such as *Oh, God*.

Burns' friend also found success in show business. Although he first had to change his name and give up pantomime for acting, Cary Grant's acting career would be filled with much greater acclaim than he ever achieved with the acrobatic troupe.

Like Burns, he appreciated an inexpensive meal. Even after he became a wildly popular—and rich—movie star, Cary Grant was notoriously frugal. During the summer of 1960, Cary Grant was filming *The Grass is Greener*. He became friendly with one of the actors in the cast, Moray Watson. Although Grant was dieting, he invited young Watson to lunch.

On the menu:

Poached Eggs

Bacon

The film also featured Deborah Kerr, Robert Mitchum and Jean Simmons. It did not achieve the success associated with some other Grant films, among them *An Affair to Remember, North by Northwest* and *To Catch a Thief.*

George Bush and Bill Clinton…

COMING FROM A FAMILY with a long tradition of public service, George Herbert Walker Bush had been a decorated WWII pilot, Congressman, United Nations Ambassador, CIA Director and a variety of high-level political appointments. As Vice President of the United States during the Reagan administration, George Bush was often called upon to host various dignitaries, diplomats and politicians.

On July 10, 1983, he was hosting a governor's conference. One of the attendees was Arkansas Governor Bill Clinton, who had first been elected as the nation's youngest governor back in 1978. He was just thirty-two years old, in his first term of what would eventually be four terms as governor.

On this day, Governor Clinton and his young family—wife Hillary and daughter Chelsea were with him—were enjoying the conference. The first meeting of the two future presidents' families was at a clambake at Bush's personal retreat in Walker's Point, Maine.

On the menu:

—— ❧ ——

Clams · Lobster
Hamburgers & Hot Dogs
Corn · Cole Slaw
Tossed Salad
Ice Cream Bars

—— ❧ ——

Bush went on to complete two terms as Ronald Reagan's Vice President. He was elected as the forty-first President of the United States, serving from 1989-1993. His term in office was filled with enormous diplomatic and military triumphs, highlighted by the ending of the Cold War and victory in the Gulf War. At the close of the Gulf War, President Bush's popularity was at an all-time high; political pundits made Bush a shoe-in for re-election. Domestically, however, the president faced a worsening economy and huge budget deficits.

President George Bush at another family picnic, this one including his son, future President George W. Bush. (George W. is at the far right, behind the barbecue grill.) Photo courtesy George Bush Library.

Meanwhile, the relatively unknown Clinton won the Democratic Party nomination to challenge Bush. With the slogan, "It's the economy, stupid!" as his personal mantra, William Jefferson Clinton upset President Bush in the 1992 election to become the forty-second President. For the next eight years, the nation enjoyed a time of unprecedented economic prosperity. Although slowed by repeated investigations into alleged personal indiscretions, President Clinton maintained his personal popularity with the voters. Even his impeachment over his actions surrounding an affair with a White House intern failed to dampen huge approval ratings.

Constitutionally barred from running for a third term, Clinton left office on January 20, 2001. His successor: President Bush's eldest son, George Walker Bush.

…and George W. Bush

George W.'s election over Bill Clinton's hand-picked successor and former Vice President Al Gore was a triumph on a number of levels. As a politician, the presidency is the highest office in the land. As an ideologue, the election marked a resurgence and reaffirmation of his conservative beliefs. Perhaps sweetest of all was the personal satisfaction George W. must have felt in defeating the administration that had ousted his father.

On December 19, 2000, President-elect Bush visited President Clinton in the White House. Eight years earlier, President-elect Clinton had a similar meeting with Bush's father. This time, the younger Bush was entering President Clinton's home. The two men settled in for lunch in the Old Family Dining Room on the second, private floor of the White House.

On the menu:

— ✣ —

Squash Soup • Greek Salad
Filet Mignon
Upside-down Apple Tart with Maple Ice Cream

— ✣ —

The two men met for over two hours. President-elect Bush, even though entering in triumph, was aware that his victory was a narrow and controversial one, and he commented that he was "here to listen" to his long-time political adversary. Bush was all too aware of the divisive nature of the long election contest and was determined to enter office as President of all the people. Coupled with a public meeting with just-defeated foe Vice President Gore, the luncheon was a visible and positive first step.

Jimmy Carter

The President and his wife dance at his Inaugural Ball, hours before gathering the family for a private breakfast feast. Photo courtesy Jimmy Carter Library.

THE THIRTY-NINTH President of the United States is a man of uncommon grace. Unfailingly polite, he said he wanted to make the government "competent and compassionate" as he attempted to improve the poor economic climate of the times and establish an effective energy policy for the nation.

The Georgia governor was unknown on the national stage when he launched his campaign for the presidency some two years before the 1976 election. Almost no one predicted that the former peanut farmer would capture the Democratic nomination. He did, of course, and went on to defeat President Gerald Ford in an extremely close vote. The American people were initially thrilled with the plainspoken man from Plains, Georgia and looked forward to a White House filled with a Southern charm unseen in the 20th Century.

Carter's inauguration immediately set the tone for his leadership style. He and his family rejected the traditional limousine ride from the Capitol steps to the White House; they walked down Pennsylvania Avenue along the parade route to their new home. He was determined to reject the trappings of an "imperial Presidency" that many associated with the recent Nixon era.

That night, President Carter, wife Rosalyn and daughter Amy were joined at the White House by the Carter's grown children and their families. They gathered early the next morning for their first "private" meal prepared by the White House chefs.

Although the Carter's had lived in the Georgia Governor's Mansion and certainly knew that their meals would be prepared for them in the White House, they were delighted at the feast the chefs had prepared for their family breakfast.

On the menu:

— ❧ —

Strawberries • Grapefruit
Eggs (scrambled, fried and poached)
Sausage, Bacon and Ham
Grits

— ❧ —

President Carter struggled to right the economy as America suffered through a recession. His emphasis in foreign policy on human rights was not as well received as it might be today. However, he did broker the historic Camp David Accords, bringing a framework of peace and hope to the Middle East. He successfully obtained ratification of the Panama Canal treaties, created the Department of Education and increased the National Park system.

Ultimately, the seizure of the American embassy staff in Iran overshadowed all of the President's initiatives and doomed his bid for re-election. Carter refused to go out on the campaign trail, preferring to stay in Washington and attempt to resolve the Iranian crisis. Ultimately, the entire embassy staff was safely freed but the release was orchestrated by the Iranians to occur immediately upon the inauguration of Ronald Reagan, Carter's successor.

In "retirement" Carter established the non-profit Carter Center in Atlanta to promote peace and human rights throughout the world. He is tireless in his efforts to observe and support fair elections around the globe as he consistently supports urban renewal and improved health care for all in the U.S.

President Carter and the First Lady found that quiet, simple meals alone were one of the few ways they could find some private moments together. Photo courtesy Jimmy Carter Library.

Fidel Castro...

AS THE TWENTY-FIRST CENTURY DAWNS, Fidel Castro remains one of the most prominent leaders in the world. His Cuban brand of communism has troubled America for forty years. Despite the fall of communism around the world and severe economic problems at home, Castro remains firmly in control as the undisputed ruler of his nation.

In 1956, however, he was the leader of a ragtag band of revolutionaries. Exiled from Batista's Cuba in July of 1955, he traveled relentlessly between the United States and Mexico to raise money, recruit and train his guerilla army. He allowed himself no liquor; no dating. His only respite from the fledgling revolution was occasional visits to Social Security Stadium in Mexico City to take in a baseball game.

He attended those games with Mike Calzadilla, a fellow Cuban who was then head of the Mexican Professional Baseball League. After the game, Castro would go to Calzadilla's home for a meal.

On the menu most nights:

Ox Tail with Capers
Olives

Castro and his friend would talk baseball into the night. Even today, almost fifty years later, baseball remains Fidel Castro's favorite, as it is unquestionably the Cuban national sport. In the international athletic community, Cuba's teams are perennial powers in Olympic competition and exhibitions with U.S. Major League baseball teams and a source of immense national pride.

... and John F. Kennedy Jr.

Photo courtesy NASA.

If the United States had a royal family, John F. Kennedy Jr. would have been our Crown Prince. From his frolics as a toddler in the White House to the searing image of his salute for his assassinated father's funeral cortege, from youthful forays into acting at Brown University and a stint as assistant New York prosecutor, America watched JFK Jr. grow into his celebrity and begin to find his place in the world.

He founded *George*, a mainstream magazine designed to appeal to a mass audience and explore the personalities in the political world. It was a perfect forum for the charismatic Kennedy; *George* was a high profile, non-controversial magazine at the center of the world political stage. A popular, regular feature of the magazine was Kennedy's monthly interview with a wide variety of people from politics, the arts or history.

In late October 1997, JFK Jr. traveled to Cuba to interview Fidel Castro, still ruler of the communist republic off the coast of Florida. Castro had first entered the American conscience around the same time as JFK Jr.'s father rose to prominence in the late '50s.

President John Kennedy had encountered Castro during the Cuban Missile Crisis and, before that, during the Bay of Pigs fiasco. Each of those events has entered American lore; the missile crisis was one of the seminal events of the Cold War and the Bay of Pigs still influences the Cuban-American people. Kennedy's father and Fidel Castro will remain forever linked in history.

When JFK Jr. and his small group of *George* magazine colleagues arrived in Cuba, then, they were unsure of when or even if they would be granted a meeting with the Cuban dictator. They waited for five days. Finally, they were escorted to a nine o'clock dinner at the Council of Ministers building in Havana. As the evening began, a waiter delivered a tray of martinis, rum, whiskey, mango juice and wine.

On the menu:

— ❧ —

Grapefruit

Consomme

Shrimp

Chicken

Ice cream

— ❧ —

Castro expressed his admiration for JFK Sr. and expressed his belief that Cuban-American relations would be vastly different had the president lived. Castro's opinions were delivered over the five-hour dinner; his public speeches are legendary for their length and his private discourses are no shorter. *George* magazine writer Inigo Thomas, who attended the meeting, reported that Kennedy was not allowed to bring a tape recorder or briefing books and was politely told that Castro considered the meal to be a private one. The result was a historic, yet oddly personal meeting between the two men.

In another cruel twist of fate to have befallen the famous Kennedy family, John F. Kennedy, Jr. lost his life when a plane he was piloting crashed less than two years after this meeting. He died on July 16, 1999.

Patsy Cline

The tragic death of Patsy Cline has only added an additional blanket of truth to the songs of sadness, love and heartache so familiar to music fans around the world. Her hit records such as "Crazy" and "I Fall to Pieces" remain music standards long after her death.

On March 5, 1963, Patsy Cline was returning from a benefit concert in Kansas City to her home in Tennessee. Along with several others, including her manager, Ms. Cline was killed when the small plane they were traveling in crashed.

The wake was held inside her home, where Patsy's husband laid her gold-lined casket in front of the living room picture window. It had been her favorite view. Stunned, somber and grieving friends and family rallied around Patsy's husband and young children. Dottie West and Loretta Lynn carved the ham. Loretta's husband Mooney and Del Wood served scrambled eggs and bacon, Roger Miller and Ann Tant served hot biscuits. Hank and Shirley Cochran brought trays of ham, chicken and sandwiches. Faron Young helped spike the drinks for anyone who asked.

On the menu:

— ❧ —

Ham
Potato Salad
Scrambled Eggs & Bacon
Ham, Chicken & Sandwich Trays
Biscuits
Iced Tea, "Spiked" drinks

— ❧ —

The double album "The Patsy Cline Story" was released after her death, and proved to be a monster hit. In addition to "Crazy" and "I Fall to Pieces," the album included "Walking After Midnight," "She's Got You" and "Sweet Dreams." In 1973, Patsy Cline became the first female singer elected to the Country Music Hall of Fame.

Jane Fonda & Ted Turner

THE MARRIAGE of Jane Fonda, left-wing activist, and Ted Turner, Southern billionaire, was as unlikely as the pairing of the star of *Barbarella* with the founder of CNN or prominent anti-war protester with the owner of the Atlanta Braves. Yet Fonda and Turner are all of those things, and many more. Turner is the largest individual landowner in the United States. Fonda's exercise videos are still the best-selling videos of all time.

They were married at Turner's Avalon estate east of Tallahassee, Florida on December 21, 1991. It was Jane's fifty-fourth birthday. The wedding feast reflected their interest in nature and wild game.

On the menu:

—— ❧ ——

Pheasant

Sweet Potatoes

Wild Rice

—— ❧ ——

Unfortunately, this power couple for the nineties did not survive as they entered the 21st century. By 2001, Jane's divorce petition citing a marriage "irretrievably broken" was filed. Her deep commitment to Christianity and Ted's well known atheism were reported to be significant factors in their break-up.

Gary Gilmore

Gary Gilmore was a lifelong criminal, finally convicted and sentenced to death for the murder of two men during a Utah robbery. After many years without state executions, Gilmore was the first to die under Utah's new death penalty statute.

His case became a *cause celebre* when Gilmore opposed delays in carrying out his sentence and sought legal help in speeding the execution. He gained even more exposure and ignited more controversy when he chose the firing squad as his method of execution, something that had not happened for many, many years.

His execution was scheduled for the night of January 16, 1977. That night, a party of sorts—Gilmore's legal team, his relatives and media representatives—gathered at the prison to support him. For a last meal, the lawyers brought in Pizza Hut pizzas with ham, salami and pepperoni. The guards confiscated the beer purchased to accompany the pizza. Everyone but Gilmore was allowed to eat. (Gilmore had not requested the pizza earlier as prison regulations required.) Against Gilmore's wishes, a stay of execution was granted.

By the time the stay was lifted, it was the next day. Gilmore was served a last meal at 4:07 p.m. before he was led to the firing squad on January 17.

On the menu:

Steak • Bread & Butter Peas
Cherry Pie • Coffee and Milk

Gilmore's death by firing squad was the last in this country. The book *Executioner's Song* won the Nobel Prize for author Norman Mailer and researcher Lawrence Schiller. Today Mailer remains one of the most well known authors in the country. Schiller continues to publish and remain involved in high profile celebrity legal proceedings, from the O.J. Simpson trial to the Jon Benet Ramsay case.

Ulysses S. Grant

Photo courtesy Still Pictures Branch, National Archives.

U.S. GRANT (1822-1885) rose from humble beginnings to become the Commander of the Union Armies during the Civil War and 18th President of the United States. Although he was often portrayed as a hard drinking, unimposing character, he was actually a modest, devoted family man whose iron will and bold military strategy propelled the Union to victory in the Civil War.

President Lincoln had become increasingly frustrated as a series of generals failed to use the superior resources of the North to defeat the Confederate forces. He finally turned to U.S. "Unconditional Surrender" Grant. Despite some setbacks, Grant never retreated after a defeat or rested after a victory. His strategy won the war.

His two terms in the White House are generally acknowledged as ineffective. Although never personally implicated, there was widespread corruption throughout his term in office. Virtually penniless in retirement, he completed his memoirs on his deathbed. It was a bestseller that supported his wife handsomely until her death in 1902; it remains one of the most highly regarded military memoirs ever written.

Grant's daughter Nellie was married on May 21, 1874. Nellie was clearly the President's favorite child; he cheerfully spoiled his only daughter. Nevertheless, he strenuously opposed this marriage to young Algernon Sartoris, an Englishman he found to be rather pompous and vain. Nellie was only eighteen and Grant hated the idea of her living in England, far from her family. As stubborn as she was spoiled, however, the nuptials went on as planned.

Her White House wedding turned out to be one of the most festive and celebrated occasions since the end of the Civil War. Only President Grant, it seemed, was distraught. After the marriage ceremony, servants searched the White House for him. He was discovered upstairs, sobbing unashamedly into Nellie's bedroom pillow. Downstairs, a wedding luncheon was served in the White House State Dining Room.

On the menu that day:

— ❧ —

Soft Crabs on Toast
Chicken Croquettes with Fresh Peas
Aspic of Beef Tongue
Broiled Spring Chicken
Strawberries & Cream
Ice cream & Ices
Wedding Cake
Fancy Cakes
Chocolate
Punch Coffee

— ❧ —

Many of Grant's post-wedding letters to his daughter survive. In them, he never fails to politely inquire about his son-in-law, but he also frequently urges her to return to the United States and raise her children as U.S. citizens. Nellie eventually divorced Sartoris and did just that; sadly, it wasn't until after Grant's death from throat cancer in 1885.

Sammy "The Bull" Gravano

SAMMY "THE BULL" GRAVANO is the violent Mafia underboss turned government informant whose testimony helped put John Gotti and scores of other Mafia bosses in jail. Gotti was the head of the Gambino crime family and was known as the "Teflon don" for his ability to avoid conviction in numerous attempts by law enforcement to prosecute him. With Gravano's testimony supporting the Government's case against him, Gotti was sentenced to multiple life sentences. Gravanno, who admitted his involvement in nineteen murders among many other crimes, served less than five years in jail, received plastic surgery and admittance into the Federal Witness Protection Program.

Gravano's intimate knowledge of the inner workings of the Mafia had been gained as he robbed, cheated, bullied and murdered his way up through the organization. But in 1970, he was a young man in his mid-twenties, still more hoodlum than Mafia tough. He was hanging out and having fun at places like Coney Island, where he met the teenaged Debra Scibetta on an outing with her older sister and a carload of friends. They spent the evening enjoying the amusement rides and eating Nathan's hot dogs.

For their first "proper" date, Debbie cooked dinner at her home.

On the menu:

Tomato Sauce
Italian Sausage
Macaroni

Their romance blossomed quickly from that point and the couple was married the next year, in April 1971. Until his conviction, Debbie and Sammy raised two children and lived a luxurious life as he moved up in the Mafia.

After he got out of jail, he left the Witness Protection Program and started a swimming pool and general construction company in Arizona. It seemed as though Gravanno had truly left his old life far behind. Although estranged, Debbie and Sammy relocated to Arizona, along with both of their now grown children.

However, the entire family was indicted on an array of drug charges. Sammy Bull once ridiculed his former boss for bringing his family into the business. Now Gravanno and his family were charged with being principles in the sale and distribution of the designer drug Ecstasy in Phoenix. The highest ranking member ever to turn Mafia rat had finally himself been "ratted out" as law enforcement officials built their case against the Gravanno family with a series of wiretaps and other evidence provided largely by informants.

Katherine Hepburn & Spencer Tracy

Together, Katherine Hepburn and Spencer Tracy were one of Hollywood's most enduring couples. Separately, they were two of the most famous movie stars in the world. Because Tracy, a Roman Catholic, was already married, the couple never publicly acknowledged their relationship. However, they did entertain and live together.

Their home was a cottage Tracy rented on George Cukor's estate outside Hollywood. Their life, especially in the cottage, was very much the stereotypical male/female relationship of the times. Hepburn doted on Tracy. She took care of all of the household chores and did the cooking.

In 1960, Tracy was starring in a movie directed by Stanley Kramer. The movie, *Inherit the Wind,* was based on the 1925 Scopes Monkey trial where famed lawyers Clarence Darrow and William Jennings Bryan faced off about the right to teach evolution in the public school system. Spencer Tracy filled the Darrow role; Frederick March filled the role based on the William Jennings Bryan character.

After work, Tracy would sometimes bring his good friend Kramer home for dinner. On those occasions, Katherine Hepburn generally prepared Tracy's favorite meal.

On the menu:

— ❧ —

Tossed Salad
Grilled Steak
Hot Fudge Sundae

— ❧ —

The movie is now regarded as one of the Hollywood classics. Katherine Hepburn and Spencer Tracy remained together until Tracy's death following the filming of *Guess Who's Coming To Dinner,* coincidentally another Stanley Kramer-directed classic.

Thomas Jefferson

Photo courtesy NARA.

THOMAS JEFFERSON was truly the first American Renaissance Man. Governor of Virginia, Minister to France, Secretary of State, Vice President, 3rd President of the United States. Author of the Declaration of Independence, founder of the University of Virginia, lawyer, gentleman farmer, noted architect and gourmet.

Jefferson was a lifelong champion of individual liberties and freedom for his country and his state. He was elected as the third President of the United States, serving two terms beginning in

1801. In 1802 Jefferson was less than one year into his first term; the threat of the French Revolution had subsided; he was in the process of slashing our military budgets, eliminating the unpopular whiskey tax and reducing our national deficit by more than a third.

A widower, President Jefferson often hosted small dinner parties consisting of friends, congressmen and other colleagues. His interest in food and wine was sparked during his stint as Minister of France and back home at Monticello, his farm. One such meal took place on February 6. Manasseh Cutler, a congressman from Massachusetts, and several others attended the meal, which began at 4 p.m. In the style of the day, the meal was laden with several different types and cuts of meat.

On the menu:

———

Rice Soup
Round of Beef
Turkey, Mutton, Ham
Loin of Veal
Mutton Cutlets
Fried Eggs, Fried Beef
Macaroni Pie
Ice Cream with a Crust of Dried Flakes
Pudding with Cream Sauce
Fresh Fruits
Wine

———

The following year saw the Louisiana Purchase, probably the finest real estate transaction in American history. Jefferson purchased the 500+ million acre transaction for $15 million—less than 3 cents per acre! Passage and repeal of the Embargo Act, the deadly duel between Alexander Hamilton and Aaron Burr and the Northwest exploration of Lewis and Clark all happened during the remainder of Jefferson's term. Each has become a part of our nation's lore.

Jefferson retired to his beloved Monticello and spent the remainder of his life writing and designing, working on his farm and his plans for the University of Virginia. He died on July 4, 1826—the same day as John Adams.

Grace Kelly

As 1955 drew to a close, Grace Kelly was one of the most accomplished and desired actresses in the world. Her film credits included *High Noon, Dial M for Murder, Rear Window* and *To Catch a Thief*. Her signature role was in *The Philadelphia Story*; she won an Oscar for her role in the film *The Country Girl*.

Her romantic life was the subject of much speculation and as varied as her film career. Among others, she had been linked to Oleg Cassini, Clark Gable, Ray Milland and William Holden. But Grace Kelly was about to give up her position as a member of Hollywood royalty for the real thing. She was in love with the handsome Prince Ranier of Monaco. Her storybook wedding and reign as Princess Grace of Monaco enthralled the world.

On this day, December 29, 1955, Grace Kelly was just another young woman talking with her best friend and sharing her exciting news. She met with Judy Kanter for lunch; Kanter knew, of course, about the romance. But the engagement had just been publicly announced the previous day and the future princess was eager to share the details with her friend.

On the menu:

Tossed Green Salad
Chicken Sandwiches
Iced Tea

The 1956 wedding of Grace Kelly and Prince Rainier was the social event of the year. Prince Ranier and Princess Grace had three children—Caroline, Albert and Stephanie. Princess Grace became the President of the Red Cross, Monaco's principal charity. She used her Hollywood connections to raise money and awareness for both the Red Cross and her principality. She remained very much at the center of the world's stage until her tragic death in a car accident on September 13, 1982.

John F. Kennedy…

After breakfast, President and Mrs. Kennedy went to Dallas for the fateful motorcade. Photo courtesy John F. Kennedy Library.

JOHN FITZGERALD KENNEDY entered the White House with a glittering resume: best-selling author (*While England Slept, Profiles in Courage,*) decorated WWII Navy hero, congressman and senator from Massachusetts. He was the shining star of one of America's most famous families. Family patriarch Joe Kennedy was a former ambassador to Great Britain and wealthy entrepreneur. JFK's maternal grandfather, for whom he was named, was a former mayor of Boston and legendary character in Massachusetts political circles.

Kennedy's presidency was filled with promise, yet marked by missteps. The Bay of Pigs, our early involvement in Viet Nam and tentative early support of the Civil Rights movement all slowed JFK's early promise. By 1963, however, Kennedy had emerged as a true world leader for his handling of the Cuban Missile Crisis and his famed speech chastising the USSR at the Berlin Wall. He had finally energized the nation with his spirited support of civil rights and our fledgling space program; he founded the Peace Corps.

On November 21, 1963, John F. Kennedy was in Texas for a series of political appearances. He had arrived in the state the night before and was thrilled with the reception he had received. He awoke early in the Texas Hotel in Fort Worth and went downstairs where he gave a brief speech to an assembled group of local dignitaries and enjoyed a breakfast in his honor.

On the menu:

Soft-Boiled Eggs

Bacon

Toast with Marmalade

Orange Juice

Coffee

After the breakfast, President Kennedy went on to Dallas. He rode with wife Jacqueline and Governor and Mrs. John Connally in an open-air limousine. As the parade passed cheering crowds and the Texas Book Depository, shots rang out. A short time later, President John Fitzgerald Kennedy was pronounced dead.

Grief, shock, confusion and outrage quickly consumed the nation. Lee Harvey Oswald was arrested for the assassination; a man named Jack Ruby killed Oswald as he was being led to a court appearance. President Johnson appointed a commission headed by Chief Justice Warren (the Warren Commission) to answer and evaluate any questions surrounding the assassination and subsequent events. This definitive investigation instead only fueled the many conspiracy theories about JFK's death that persist today.

As time marches inevitably forward, the shocking assassination of our 35th President remains forever frozen as one of the defining moments in 20th century American history. His legacy of courage and inspired leadership in the face of adversity still remains for millions of people throughout the world.

... and P. J. Nehru

President Kennedy was a great admirer of Pandit Jawaharlal Nehru, Prime Minister of India, even before he was elected to the presidency. Once elected, JFK was determined to reach out to India, then emerging as an Asian power. Nehru was received on an official state visit in November 1961.

Prime Minister Nehru and Madame Gandhi met the President and First Lady Jacqueline Kennedy in Newport, Rhode Island before going on to visit Disneyland in California. In a nod to Indian custom, the guests were served identical meals but President Kennedy and Nehru were served their meals on a separate floor from Mrs. Kennedy and Madame Gandhi.

On the menu:

— ❧ —

New England Clam Chowder
Cailles Veronique (Quail in Grape Sauce)
Glazed Carrots & Mimosa Salad
Bavarian Cream Mold with Oranges
Petit Fours with Almonds
Demitasse

— ❧ —

It was a terrific menu. The same cannot be said for the meeting. Kennedy was aware of India's emerging policy of non-alignment but was impressed with Nehru's idealism and economic reforms, and had high hopes for the Asian country's friendship as a counterbalance in the region to communist China. His hopes were not realized, although no real damage was done to U.S.-India relations. Nehru was distant and brief in his reaction to the charismatic Kennedy's overtures. Kennedy himself later called the meeting "the worst state visit I have had."

Robert E. Lee

Confederate winter headquarters 1862. Photo courtesy Library of Congress.

ROBERT E. LEE (1807-1870), commander of the Confederate Army, is thought by many to be the greatest American soldier. At the outbreak of the Civil War, Lee struggled to choose sides. A West Point graduate and distinguished veteran of the Spanish-American War, Lee was descended from one of America's most famous families. His father was Revolutionary War hero Light Horse Harry Lee.

Unwilling to leave his beloved Virginia, Lee decided to join the Confederates and resigned his U.S. Army commission. After a rocky start, Lee assumed command of the armies. Despite being out-manned, ill-equipped and under-funded, Lee led the Confederates to a string of spectacular victories.

It was Christmas day, 1862.

Stewards at General Stonewall Jackson's camp began serious preparation for the afternoon feast. Not only was it Christmas day, but the general expected a guest list that included Generals Pendleton, Stuart and von Borcke. The guest of honor was his boss, General Robert E. Lee. It was a special day, and Jackson's camp bustled with activity.

In four short months, Stonewall Jackson would be dead; Lee himself would hint that Jackson's death at Chancellorsville was the beginning of the end for the Confederacy. This, however, was a time of hope in the South, a time when all things were still possible. In his Moss Neck headquarters on the banks of the Rappahannock River in Virginia, Jackson's men had even secured a supply of butter, perhaps the rarest of treats in the entire Confederacy.

In addition to butter, the menu read as follows:

Pails of Oysters

Turkeys • Ham

Biscuits

Pickles

Cake • Wine

Just six months after this meal, defeat at Gettysburg would begin the long slide to the South's ultimate surrender. Nevertheless, after the war, Lee was the unquestioned hero of the South. He accepted defeat with uncommon grace and dignity; offered untold riches for a variety of jobs, Lee chose instead to accept the presidency of what became Washington and Lee University. He believed it his duty to help educate and guide the nation's youth through the post-war years. He died in 1870.

Abraham Lincoln

Lincoln's words, seen reproduced here on a WWII poster, continue to lead and inspire the American people. Photo courtesy NARA.

ABRAHAM LINCOLN was elected the sixteenth President of the United States. He is best known, of course, as the leader of the country during the Civil War. Lincoln's Emancipation Proclamation is credited as being the speech that finally and formally ended legal slavery in this country. His steady leadership and courage led the Union to the final victory over the Confederacy and reunited the United States. His tragic assassination cut short his second term, but he did live to see the end of the Civil War.

Abe Lincoln was perhaps our greatest president, but he entered office as a partisan politician in the most divisive period in our history. By the time of his inaugural, the Confederacy was already a reality; in fact, Jefferson Davis had been inaugurated as its president two weeks earlier. Lincoln arrived in Washington via a secret route and under guard, but he insisted on traveling to his swearing-in ceremony at the Capitol in an open-air carriage, along with President Buchanan.

Lincoln's inaugural address was a failed attempt to reassure the South that he had no plans or interest in interfering with individual state's rights, including the right to keep slaves. He quoted portions of the Republican Party platform that repudiated any interference in the operation of any state's domestic institutions. Lincoln left no doubt about whom he considered the aggressors in this dispute, however, nor any doubt about his determination to protect the Union. He said, "You can have no conflict without being yourselves the aggressors. You have no oath registered in heaven to destroy the Government, while I shall have the most solemn one to 'preserve, protect and defend it.'"

It was Monday, March 4, 1961. Soon enough, shots would be fired at Fort Sumter and the Civil War would consume the nation. But this day was Lincoln's to assume the highest office in the land. After ceremonies at the Capitol Building, Lincoln and his party moved to the Willard Hotel for an inaugural luncheon.

On the menu that day:

— ❧ —

Mock Turtle Soup
Corned Beef and Cabbage
Parsley Potatoes
Blackberry Pie
Coffee

— ❧ —

Lincoln and his family moved directly from the Willard Hotel into the White House. For the next five years, Lincoln led the nation with courage and conviction. Most historians rate his presidential performance as among the best in U.S. history. Unfortunately, he paid for that performance with his life when John Wilkes Booth assassinated him shortly after the end of the Civil War in 1865.

Marilyn Monroe

Photo courtesy NARA.

NORMA JEANE MORTENSON was born June 1, 1926, in Los Angeles, California. Baptized as Norma Jeane Baker, she never knew her father; mother Gladys suffered from mental problems. Consequently, much of her youth was spent in foster homes and orphanages.

Finally, a job as a photographer's model led to a career as a movie actress. As Marilyn Monroe, her career really took off in the '50s, beginning with bit parts in *The Asphalt Jungle* and *All About*

Eve. Between 1953 and 1955, Monroe starred in *Gentlemen Prefer Blondes, How to Marry a Millionaire* and *The Seven Year Itch*.

She was widely known as one of the sexiest and most desirable women on earth. She was one of the first actresses whose every move was chronicled by reporters and photographers. Her marriages, especially to Joe DiMaggio and Arthur Miller, were closely scrutinized as her career continued in the late fifties with *Bus Stop* 1956, *Some Like It Hot* 1959 and *The Misfits* 1961.

Her premature death in 1962 was ruled an overdose of sleeping pills. Rumors of her affairs with the Kennedy brothers and hints of murder/conspiracy have only increased her legend.

In the late '40s, Marilyn Monroe was working as a model. She had already appeared on over thirty major magazine covers and signed a contract with Twentieth Century-Fox, but she was not yet a movie star.

On May 27, 1949, she reported to her modeling assignment with photographer Thomas Kelly and his wife. The results of their work that day would include the now famous nude centerfold shot of Marilyn sprawled on a red bedspread. At that moment, however, Marilyn Monroe was broke. The $50 payment for her work just covered her overdue rent.

Marilyn hadn't eaten. Kelly and his wife took her out for chili, her first and only meal of the day.

Her menu:

— ❧ —

Chili

— ❧ —

Richard Nixon

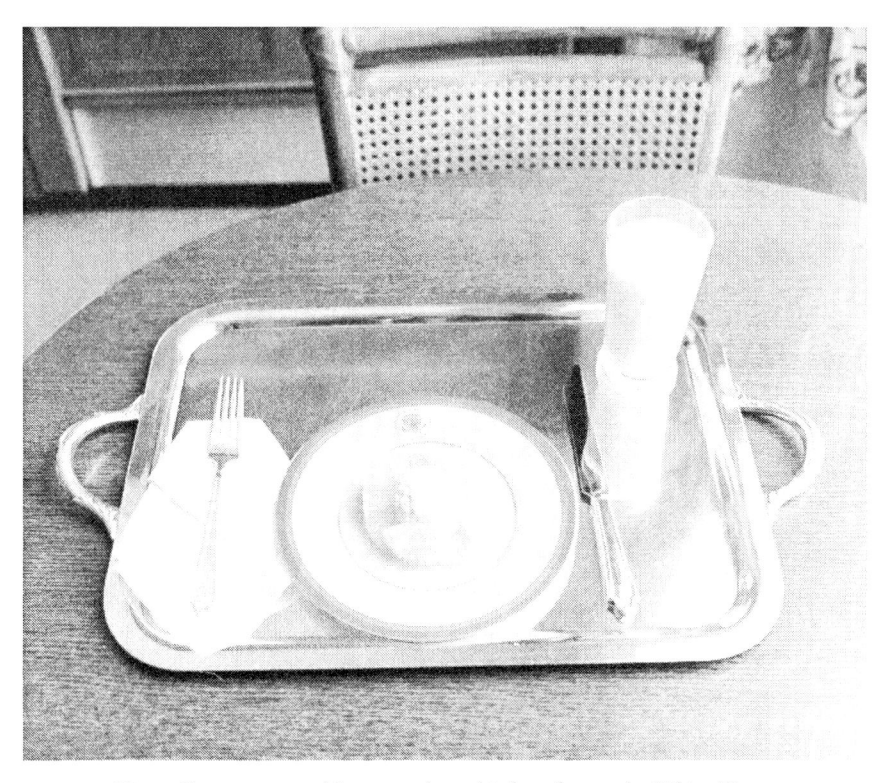

Virtually every move Nixon made on his last day at the White House was photographed. His last meal was no exception. Photo courtesy Nixon Presidential Materials Project.

IN 1968, REPUBLICAN CANDIDATE Richard M. Nixon was elected the 37th President of the United States. His election capped one of the greatest comebacks in American political history. Nixon had been a popular member of Congress as both a Senator and Representative. He was elected Vice-President of the United States for two terms under President Eisenhower. In 1960, however, he was defeated by JFK in a bid for the presidency and then defeated in the race to be elected governor of California. He temporarily retired from politics.

His 1968 election was a huge surprise; many called it a resurrection. As president, Nixon became known as a foreign policy genius; he presided over the end of the Vietnam War, opened relations with China and improved relations with the Soviet Union during the Cold War.

President Nixon was a lightning rod for the times; he was vilified by the liberals, scorned by the Flower Power generation and staunchly defended by conservatives. His landslide victory in the 1972 election contest was preceded by a barely noticed break-in at the Democratic Party headquarters. Those headquarters were in a new hotel complex known as the Watergate.

"Watergate" led to Nixon's downfall. The American public was shocked at the sordid tale of lies and deception heard on secret White House recordings Nixon himself made. Nixon's participation in the cover-up of the affair led to impeachment hearings and his subsequent resignation.

On August 8, 1974, Richard Nixon became the first president of the United States to resign from office. At 8:30 a.m. that morning, President Nixon had his regular breakfast of cold cereal, orange juice and milk. He spent the rest of the morning working on his resignation speech, getting his haircut and making a few calls. He met with Vice-President Ford and a congressional delegation.

In the White House mess, Thursday was Mexican lunch day. Nixon's staff members munched on tacos and other assorted Mexican dishes. At 9 p.m. that night, Nixon gave his resignation speech to the public, met with his family and then Al Haig, his Chief of Staff.

His last day in office was August 9. His speech the previous evening left the nation bitterly divided. He was determined to leave his office with his head up and dignity intact. Alone, he ordered his last meal as President.

On the menu:

— ❧ —

Pineapple Slices
Milk
Cottage Cheese

— ❧ —

The disgraced Nixon flew home to California. For the rest of his life, he remained a controversial figure, but his foreign policy writings and political savvy restored some luster to his reputation in his later years. He died on April 22, 1994.

Elvis Presley...

Photo courtesy Nixon Presidential Materials Project.

IN LATE 1957, Elvis Presley was the King of Rock and Roll, but he was determined to become the King of Hollywood. He moved into the top floor of the Roosevelt Hotel during the filming of the movie *King Creole*.

Crowds followed Elvis everywhere; going out was so difficult, Elvis was virtually trapped in the hotel. That was part of the reason he traveled with an entourage of old buddies, his "Memphis Mafia." In the evenings, after a long day of filming, Elvis would order in and have small parties with his boisterous but basically well-behaved friends.

On the menu:

— ❦ —

Hamburgers
Hot Dogs
Pizza
Potato Chips
Malted Milk Shakes & Cokes

— ❦ —

... and Natalie Wood

JUST HOME FROM THE ARMY in the early 1960's, Elvis Presley went back to Hollywood to pursue his dream of movie stardom. While he was out there, he began dating Natalie Wood. She was talented, beautiful, sophisticated and already a veteran movie star.

Natalie Wood had been earning a living in the movies since she began as a 4-year-old child actress with a small part in the movie *Happy Land*. From *Miracle on 34th Street* to *Rebel Without a Cause* and *West Side Story*, Wood starred in some of the most popular films of all time; she literally grew up on the screen. When she began dating Elvis, Natalie Wood was at the top of Hollywood's movie queen list. She found the charismatic star to be handsome, sexy—and hopelessly naïve, a true country gentleman.

On Natalie's first visit to Graceland, Elvis introduced her to his mother. Gladys prepared an elaborate Southern feast, ostensibly for Natalie Wood, but mostly to welcome her devoted son home. On the menu:

Country Ham

Black-Eyed Peas

Potatoes Fried Corn

Hominy Grits

Corn Pone Biscuits

… and The Beatles

By 1965, The Beatles were on their way to becoming the most popular recording artists in history. They had been unsuccessful in arranging a meeting with Elvis during their triumphant world tour the previous year and were anxious to try again. According to John Lennon, they finally met Elvis on August 27, 1965. Elvis was a long-time idol of the Beatles and they were both nervous and excited to meet him. Although Elvis was not overly impressed with his rivals, he was curious to meet them.

The historic meeting began, again according to Lennon, with an awkward—and awed—silence, at least from John, Paul, George and Ringo. Finally, Elvis commented that "if you're just going to sit there and stare at me, I'm going to bed." That joke broke the tension and an evening of conversation and playing music ensued. Elvis asked his cook, Alvena Roy, to prepare a midnight supper for his guests.

In her cookbook, she recalled the menu:

— ❧ —

Broiled Chicken Livers Wrapped in Bacon

Sweet and Sour Meatballs

Deviled Eggs

Cracked Crab

Cold Cuts

Fruit

Cheese

— ❧ —

Ronald Reagan…

Photo courtesy Ronald Reagan Library.

FIRST, HIS ACTING BACKGROUND and hands-off management style led his enemies to label him as a lightweight Republican shill. As former governor of California, his election was dismissed in the East as a typical fluke to be expected from that state. And even after a presidential landslide election, underestimating President Ronald Wilson Reagan was a mistake that would be repeated on a world stage throughout two terms of what came to be known as the Reagan Revolution.

His ability to inspire and energize the nation led to his nickname as the "Great Communicator." His patriotism and genuine love for the country was contagious. His consistent call for less government, lower taxes and stronger defense became a mantra for the conservative movement in the United States that lives into the 21st century.

Reagan's immediate objective upon assuming office in 1981 was to stimulate a domestic economy mired in recession. But just two months into his term, he was shot; his grace and courage in the aftermath of the unsuccessful assassination attempt united the country behind him. He introduced a program of reducing taxes and government expenditures while increasing military spending.

Reagan's foreign policy was "peace through strength." He declared war on international terrorism. His dramatic summit meetings with Soviet leader Mikhail Gorbachev led to a treaty eliminating intermediate-range nuclear missiles. He supported anti-Communist insurgencies throughout the world, most notably in Granada. President Reagan's resolve and leadership of the defense build-up are generally credited with hastening the end of the Cold War.

He left office in 1989 during a time of unprecedented peacetime prosperity. Just five years later, the 83-year-old ex-president issued one of the most poignant letters in American history when he told the world he was suffering from Alzheimer's disease. The perpetually optimistic Reagan said, in part, "I now begin the journey that will lead me into the sunset of my life. I know that for America there will always be a bright dawn ahead."

Two years later, on his 85th birthday, wife Nancy gave Reagan a special birthday gift. Many of the president's personal milestones had been celebrated at Chasen's, his favorite restaurant in the heart of the Hollywood entertainment world. The restaurant had closed almost a year earlier, but for Mr. Reagan, the restaurant re-opened for one special day.

On the menu:

— ❧ —

Scottish Smoked Salmon
Chicken Pot Pie
Coupe Snowballs
(ice cream, toasted & shredded coconut, chocolate syrup)

— ❧ —

… and Queen Elizabeth

IN 1983, NANCY REAGAN hosted a dinner for Queen Elizabeth II and her husband, Prince Philip. The dinner was at the M*A*S*H soundstage at Twentieth Century Fox in Los Angeles, home territory for Mrs. Reagan and the five hundred plus members of Hollywood royalty in attendance. Ginger Rogers and Fred Astaire, Cary Grant, Frank Sinatra and Bette Davis were among the guests who dined with the British monarch.

It was a formal affair. Mrs. Reagan was known for presenting elegant, simple menus that reflected American tastes. She again relied on the talents of Chasen's—in this instance, their catering service—to prepare the meal.

On the menu:

— ❧ —

Papaya with Bay Shrimp
Chicken Pot Pie
Fresh Spinach with Bacon
Toasted Coconut Snowball
Demitasse Wine

— ❧ —

Queen Elizabeth enjoyed the Reagans on a personal and political level. She is shown here sharing one of her favorite activities with the President. Photo courtesy Reagan Library.

...and Presidents Nixon, Ford, Carter and Bush

Just before lunch, the five men pose in the replica of the Oval Office found at the Reagan Library. Photo courtesy George Bush Library.

THE RONALD REAGAN PRESIDENTIAL LIBRARY in the California Simi Valley was dedicated on November 4, 1991. All five of the then-living presidents—Nixon, Ford, Carter, Bush and Reagan—attended the festivities with their wives. Other guests included family representatives from Presidents Roosevelt, Johnson and Kennedy, along with many other distinguished guests from politics, Hollywood and foreign dignitaries from around the world.

A luncheon was scheduled after the opening. Nixon's wife Pat became ill, however, and he was forced to leave before the luncheon. The remaining presidents led the distinguished crowd at the festive meal.

On the menu:

— ❧ —

English Sole

Chinese Peapods

New Potatoes with Basil

Toasted Coconut Ice Cream Balls

— ❧ —

Franklin Delano Roosevelt

Photo courtesy Franklin Delano Roosevelt Library.

FRANKLIN ROOSEVELT is on every list of great U.S. Presidents. He created the New Deal and is credited with leading our country out of the Great Depression. His courage after Pearl Harbor, "a day that will live in infamy…" inspired the nation as he led the country through much of World War II.

FDR often escaped Washington, D.C. by vacationing in Warm Springs, Georgia. He thoroughly enjoyed the warm waters there and found them to be therapeutic. He had been stricken with polio as a child and was mostly confined to a wheelchair, a fact that many citizens in the Radio Age didn't know.

On April 12, 1945, he was in the "Little White House" in Warm Springs. The end of World War II was in sight. His staff was busy making preparations for a festive luncheon to be held in FDR's honor later in the day. As he was most mornings, FDR was served breakfast in bed.

After his meal, FDR remained in bed. He never got up, dying of a cerebral hemorrhage before lunch.

On the menu for that final breakfast:

— ❧ —

Fried Eggs

Bacon

One Slice of Toast

— ❧ —

Paul Simon

For the last half of the 1960s, Simon and Garfunkel was one of the most successful recording duos in the world of popular music. Their first album, "The Sounds of Silence," became a classic and topped the charts. Although Paul Simon and Art Garfunkel's music together certainly endures, their partnership has been marked by repeated and prolonged separations.

The first such split began in 1970, when Paul enrolled in songwriting classes in New York and began work on a solo album. He frequented a Chinese restaurant where he became inspired by a popular menu item featuring fried chicken and scrambled eggs. The song "Mother and Child Reunion" became a cut on the February 1972 album "Paul Simon" and one of his most popular hits. It has become the unofficial anthem for *Collectible Meals*.

Frank Sinatra

Frank Sinatra was recently voted the greatest crooner of the 20th Century. He was the original teen idol and became an accomplished actor. His acting accolades included the 1954 Academy Award for his supporting role in *From Here to Eternity*. As a singer of American popular music, only Elvis Presley was his peer. Only his legendary celebrity exploits could match his astonishing talents.

Sinatra was the leader of the famed Rat Pack—Dean Martin, Sammy Davis Jr., Joey Bishop, et. al.—their adventures and his various romances with some of the world's most beautiful women kept the public enthralled for many years. His frequent appearances in Las Vegas and involvement in Reno's Cal-Neva Lodge fueled rumors of Mafia ties. His surname and tough guy persona did nothing to dissuade the rumors.

The fictional Frank Sinatra was Vito Corleone's godson and sang at Connie Corleone's wedding feast in *The Godfather*. One of the real Frank Sinatra's wedding feasts took place a couple of days after his wedding ceremony to Mia Farrow in July 1966. Frank's mother prepared a traditional Italian celebration for Frank and his new bride in her Fort Lee, New Jersey home. In attendance, among others, were Toots Shor, Jilly Rizzo, Joe E. Lewis, Rosalind Russell, Liza Minelli, Freddie Brisson and Nancy Sinatra, Jr.

On the menu:

— ❧ —

Ravioli

Scallopine

Scungilli

Stuffed Green Lasagna Noodles

Fettucine • *Corkscrew Pasta*

Macaroni • *Spaghetti*

Sausage Gnocchi

Cheese, Cold cuts

Desserts

— ❧ —

Farrow was Sinatra's third wife. She was the star of *Rosemary's Baby* and wanted to continue her acting career. In Sinatra's mind, being Mrs. Frank Sinatra was career enough; his marriage to the much younger Farrow lasted only two years. The divorce was relatively friendly.

His first marriage had been to childhood sweetheart Nancy, mother of his three children. That union ended with his romance of the beautiful actress Ava Gardner, who became his second wife in 1951. Although that marriage lasted just five years, the volatile romance with Gardner is rumored to have been the great love of his life.

Finally, in 1976, he married the woman who would devote her life to him, Barbara Marx Sinatra, widow of Zeppo Marx. She remained by his side until he suffered a fatal heart attack on May 14, 1998.

Princess Diana

Diana was the center of attention wherever she went. She is pictured here dancing with American film star John Travolta at the White House. Photo courtesy Reagan Library.

LADY DIANA SPENCER was the most famous, most recognizable, most photographed woman in the world at the time of her tragic death in 1997. As a young bride, she enthralled the world in her real—life fairy tale wedding. The world watched as she and Prince Charles raised two young princes; we watched as their marriage crumbled.

Finally, Lady Diana seemed to have found her public niche as champion of children and the underprivileged. In private, Diana was devoted to her children and had apparently finally found love with Dodi al Fayed, son of a wealthy father whose business interests included Harrod's Department Store in London and the Ritz-Carlton in Paris.

The last day of Diana's life began with a romantic breakfast on the yacht Jonikal off Sardinia's Emerald Coast in the Mediterranean. It was the last meal of a vacation that seemed to cement the love affair between the princess and Dodi al Fayed. It was a moment when all the things Diana had dreamed of finally seemed possible.

After the meal she and Dodi were planning to fly to Paris before rejoining her boys in London.

On their breakfast menu:

— ❧ —

Croissants
Basket of Fruit
(bananas, apples, grapes, oranges and kiwis)
Coffee
Orange Juice

— ❧ —

Diana had both orange juice and coffee with milk; Dodi skipped the orange juice and took his coffee black.

Tragically, they left for Paris, where they would stay one last night before returning to London. That evening in the private Imperial Suite at the Ritz Carlton, Diana and Dodi dined alone.

On the menu:

— ❧ —

for Diana:

*Asparagus & Mushroom
Omelet Appetizer
Dover Sole
with Vegetables Tempura*

for Dodi:

*Grilled Turbot
Tattinger Champagne*

— ❧ —

After finishing their meal, the famous couple began their final journey into the public spotlight, forever young.

Jimmy Stewart

If not at the top, Jimmy Stewart is in the Top Ten of every poll of great movie stars. His list of credits include *Harvey, Rear Window, Vertigo, Man Who Shot Liberty Valance, The Philadelphia Story, Mr. Smith Goes to Washington* and *It's a Wonderful Life*.

He was the first major movie star to volunteer for the armed services during WWII. He served in the Air Force, earning the Distinguished Flying Cross, Croix de Guerre and numerous battle stars. President Truman said that if he and his wife had a son, "…we'd want him to be just like Jimmy Stewart."

In the winter of 1934, however, Jimmy Stewart was not yet the famous movie star he would later become. He hung around with other, unknown young actors like Henry Fonda, auditioning for parts and learning his craft. He was a struggling young Broadway actor, six foot three inches and one hundred thirty-five pounds, trying to gain weight.

He frequented a cafeteria on Eighth Avenue in Manhattan where the 40-cent tab for his normal meal was just within his budget.

On the menu:

Beef Stew
Rice Pudding
Milk

By 1948, Stewart was still slender, but his financial situation was much improved. He was starring in Alfred Hitchcock's *Rope* for a $300,000 salary, leaving the need for 40 cent meals far behind.

Elizabeth Taylor & Richard Burton

Elizabeth Taylor, born in 1932, is a legendary dramatic actress of both the stage and screen. From childhood roles in films like *Lassie, Come Home* and *National Velvet* in the 1940s to the Broadway stage in *The Little Foxes* in 1981, Elizabeth Taylor has commanded a place at the top of America's acting/celebrity communities.

Her film credits include *Cat on a Hot Tin Roof*, *Cleopatra* and *Suddenly, Last Summer*. She won Academy Awards for *Butterfield 8* and *Who's Afraid of Virginia Woolf?*

Today, she is the premier fund-raiser for AIDS victims and primary spokesman for her own perfume. Health problems from pneumonia to a brain tumor have hampered her appearances in recent years, although she continues to accept occasional film roles.

Her personal life still commands considerable interest throughout the world. She has had eight marriages—two to Richard Burton. Indeed, Taylor's life with Burton framed her professional career and cemented her position as one of the world's foremost Hollywood stars.

Richard Burton (1925-1984) was a famed British stage and film actor known for historical roles in films including *The Robe*, *Cleopatra* and *Alexander the Great*. He was one of a long line of great British actors/leading men, although he was perhaps best known for his two marriages to Elizabeth Taylor. He starred with her in several projects including *Who's Afraid of Virginia Woolf* and *The Taming of the Shrew*.

Burton's romance of the beautiful Elizabeth Taylor unfolded during the filming of the movie *Cleopatra*. Their affair made headlines around the world.

On November 18, 1968, Elizabeth Taylor and Richard Burton were hard at work filming in Europe. Taylor was filming *The*

Only Game in Town with Warren Beatty and Burton was filming *Staircase* with Rex Harrison.

They took a weekend break from filming to spend some quiet time together. Of course, this high-profile couple got to relax a little differently from most. They decided to visit the Rothchild's at their palatial estate Chateau de Ferueres in France. They slept until noon, enjoying a late breakfast in bed.

On the menu:

— ❦ —

Bacon Eggs

Brioche

Apples

— ❦ —

A lazy afternoon was followed by high tea at 4:30 p.m.
On that menu:

— ❦ —

Chicken in the Pot with Vegetables

Various Cheeses

desserts:

Roasted Chestnuts

Raisins

Figs

Mandarin Oranges

Apples

— ❦ —

Their weekend respite from the spotlight ended all too soon. Extravagant living and heavy drinking took their toll on their life together; they married, divorced and married again. A second divorce finally ended their romance. Their stormy relationship simply could not survive their time as the world's most famous couple.

Astronaut Andrew Thomas

The shuttle returns Thomas to the United States. Photo courtesy NASA.

AUSTRALIAN BORN ASTRONAUT Andrew Thomas was the last NASA representative to live onboard the Soviet space station Mir. His return to Earth on June 12, 1998 closed three years of U.S.-Russian cooperation and paved the way for the establishment of the international space station.

Thomas' voyage lent a whole new meaning to the phrase "catching the shuttle". He arrived on Mir after riding the U.S. space shuttle Endeavor and returned to Earth 141 days later on the shuttle Discovery. Thomas lived on Mir for four and one-half months. While there, he answered a question from a group of Australian schoolchildren about food cravings by saying that roast beef would be high on his list. By the time he began his trip home, however, he changed his mind. Mission Control assured him that his requested meal would be ready.

During his extended visit to space, Thomas' body was weakened. He had to be carried from the shuttle on a recliner. He was taken to the crew's quarters at Kennedy Space Center, where his meal awaited him.

On the menu:

— ⁂ —

Lasagna
Oreo Cookie Ice Cream

— ⁂ —

The Titanic

April 14, 1912.

The night the Titanic went down has been discussed, acted, filmed and written about from almost the moment tragedy struck. Virtually every aspect of the voyage has been chronicled. An entire book, *Last Dinner on the Titanic* by Rick Archbold and Dana McCauley, is devoted to the menus of the various dining salons onboard the ship.

John Jacob Astor was probably the wealthiest and most famous passenger aboard ship that night, but he was most certainly not out of place. The maiden voyage of the luxury liner included a Who's Who of the wealthy and privileged in high society. Colleagues such as Walter Douglas, director of Quaker Oats, and financier George Widener were also on board.

Meals for the privileged during that time were elaborate, time-consuming rituals—a perfect match for transatlantic travel and a luxury liner. In the ornate first class dining saloon, passengers were enjoying a spectacular eleven-course meal. As the Titanic collided with the iceberg that sealed her doom, it is likely that most of the guests felt only a slight vibration.

Just one actual menu from the first class dining room survived that terrible night. On the menu:

— ❧ —

Various Hors d'Oeuvres
Oysters • Consomme Olga
Cream of Barley
Salmon with Mousseline Sauce • Cucumbers
Filet Mignons Lili • Chicken Lyonnaise
Vegetable Marrow Farcie
Lamb with Mint Sauce
Roast Duckling with Applesauce
Sirloin of Beef with Chateau Potatoes
Green Peas • Creamed Carrots
Boiled Rice
Parmentier & Boiled New Potatoes
Punch Romaine • Roasted Squab & Cress
Cold Asparagus with Vinaigrette
Pate de Foie Gras • Celery
Waldorf Pudding
Peaches in Chartreuse Jelly
Chocolate & Vanilla Eclairs
French Ice Cream
Assorted Fresh Fruits and Cheese
Coffee

— ❧ —

Karla Faye Tucker

Karla Faye Tucker, 38, was a born—again Christian who enlisted enormous worldwide support in her effort to be spared the death penalty which she received for her participation in the brutal ax murder of two people in 1983.

An attractive, articulate, apparently changed woman, Karla Faye Tucker was a former prostitute and drug abuser who had testified about the sexual thrill she got from her participation in two particularly gruesome murders. As the first woman in Texas to face execution since the Civil War, Ms. Tucker's case ignited a firestorm of debate about the death penalty.

President George W. Bush was then the governor of Texas. He was known as a law and order governor who strongly supported the death penalty and rarely even considered using his pardon power. Many prominent members of the religious right—prime Bush supporters—lobbied on Karla Faye Tucker's behalf, as did Pope John Paul.

Bush relied on his state parole board, however, and on February 2, 1998, Karla's final appeal to the Texas Board of Pardons and Paroles was denied. Her execution was set (and carried out) for 6 p.m. February 3. For her last meal, Karla Faye Tucker chose a simple meal.

On the menu:

— ❧ —

Banana • Peaches
Tossed Salad with Ranch or Italian Dressing

— ❧ —

Gianni Versace

If the glitz and glamour of the 1990's all came together in Miami—and it did—then Gianni Versace was the king of that world. His fashion empire was booming. He moved easily from the fashion and music scene to the jet set and European royalty to Hollywood. He was wealthy beyond his wildest dreams; his mansions around the world were legendary, most of all the $40 million renovation of his Casa Casuarina in Miami. As one of the giants of the fashion world, Versace introduced the supermodel movement, led the way with his ready-to-wear collections and bold but accessible designs.

Versace was a man of habit; he and his entourage followed a predictable routine while in Miami. One typically hot July day, Versace took his normal stroll to the News Café, some four blocks from his home on Ocean Drive. While there, he ordered breakfast.

On the menu:

— ✣ —

Two Eggs, Over-Easy
Bacon
Whole Wheat Toast
Black Coffee

— ✣ —

After his meal, Versace strolled home. As he was opening his beautiful wrought-iron gate, he was attacked, shot twice in the head, and killed. Andrew Cunanan, wanted for a vicious murder spree across the country and subject of a massive manhunt, claimed his final victim. Days later, Cunanan killed himself as police closed in on him.

Celebrities from around the world expressed their shock and grief. Diana, Princess of Wales, wept on rocker Elton John's shoulder at the funeral. Rival Calvin Klein summed up the loss. "The fashion world has lost one of the great designers of our time. Gianni created a unique style which will live on after his death."

George Washington

George Washington, depicted here at his "Farewell to Officers" luncheon. Photo of engraving courtesy NARA.

THE ACHIEVEMENTS of George Washington are best chronicled in many other places—suffice it to say that he was a giant figure in the founding of our country, the first among equals of the founding fathers. Gentleman farmer, Commanding General of the Continental Army, first President of the United States, George Washington was a true leader of our country.

November 25, 1783 was known as British Evacuation Day. It was the day to celebrate victory in the Revolutionary War. George Washington and French ambassador Luzenne presided over a huge banquet and fireworks celebration at the Fraunces Tavern in New York.

Thirteen toasts capped the evening festivities. The thirteenth toast was "May the remembrance of this day be a lesson to princes." It was a toast that foretold Washington's—and the nation's—approach and commitment to our young democracy.

On the menu:

— ❧ —

Fish House Punch

Crab Caws with Dill Mustard Sauce

Pate Maison Fraunces

Cheddar Biscuits

Sorrel Soup with Sippets

Cold Poached Striped Bass with Cucumber Sauce

White Wine • Mushroom Pastry

Beefsteak and Kidney Pie

Roasted Lamb with Oyster Forcemeat

Baked, Smoked Country Ham

Madeira Molded Wine Jelly

Yam and Chestnut Pippins

Pilau of Rice • Ragoo French Beans

Skillet Cranberries

Watermelon Pickles • Pear Honey

Sally Lunn Molded Butter Prints

Claret

Carrot Tea Cake

Tipsy Squire
Tansy Pie
Whiskey Nut Balls
Chocolate Truffles
Apples, Hazelnuts, Pears, Almonds, and Grapes
Tobacco
Coffee, Madeira, Port

— ❧ —

Fourteen years earlier, George Washington was celebrating a different, more traditional holiday at the Kenmore House in Fredericksburg, Virginia. Kenmore was the home of Fielding and Betty Lewis—George's sister—and the Washington's brought along Mother Washington to share the Christmas 1769 holiday with all of the various Lewis and Washington families in attendance.

The Christmas Day brunch was a festive and elaborately decorated meal.

On the menu:

— ❧ —

Holiday Egg Nog
Virginia Ham
Beaten Biscuits   •   Corn Pudding
Chicken and Oyster Pie
Pumpkin Chips
Cucumber Pickle

Claret
Mincemeat Pie
Filbert Pudding
Honey Flummery
Plum Pudding
Walnuts
Madeira, Coffee

Martha Washington. Photo courtesy NARA.

John Wayne

John Wayne visiting U.S. troops in Viet Nam. Photo courtesy NARA.

JOHN WAYNE (1907-1979), actor, director and producer was for many years the top box office draw in the world. Through his films, he became known as the ultimate American cowboy, soldier and hero.

His start in the film business was as an assistant prop man in a summer job arranged by his USC football coach; the director of that first film was John Ford. Wayne's friendship with the famous director would eventually lead to his starring role in the film classic *Stagecoach*. Among his other film credits: *Fort Apache, The Alamo* and *True Grit*, for which he won the 1969 Oscar.

In 1952 John Wayne was one of the biggest movie stars in the world. He was scouting film locations in Tingo Maria, Peru when he spotted Pilar, a beautiful young actress. Pilar was in town filming the otherwise forgettable movie *Green Hell*. The Duke was instantly smitten and arranged to take her to dinner that very evening at the only hotel/restaurant in Tingo Maria.

On the menu that night:

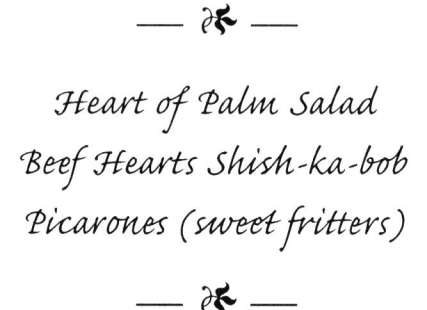

— ❧ —

Heart of Palm Salad
Beef Hearts Shish-ka-bob
Picarones (sweet fritters)

— ❧ —

Pilar soon became Wayne's third wife. John Wayne was a larger than life figure; his legendary fishing expeditions, gambling and carousing with John Ford and his other Hollywood friends foreshadowed a tempestuous relationship. They remained married, however, for twenty-five years.

He had a cancerous lung removed fifteen years before his death and spent much of the rest of his life raising money and awareness for cancer research. Fittingly, his last film was *The Shootist*, in which he played an aging gunfighter preparing for his final, fatal showdown. John Wayne died from cancer on June 11, 1979.

Mae West

AT THE AGE OF FOURTEEN, she was billed as "The Baby Vamp" in vaudeville. She was a writer whose plays included *SEX*, for which she was arrested. In her movie debut, her reply to a coat check girl who remarked "Goodness! What lovely diamonds!" was "Goodness has nothing to do with it!" Her last movie, *Sextette*, was released in 1978, two years before her death at the age of 87. For more than seventy years, Mae West titillated American audiences with her beauty and constant sexual innuendo.

In 1909, Mae West was just sixteen years old. Her mother Matilda introduced her to fellow vaudeville performer Frank Wallace. The older Wallace became Mae West's partner on the vaudeville/burlesque circuit. During their first year together, Frank and Mae held rehearsals in the basement of Matilda's house on Bushwick Avenue in New York. After rehearsal, Frank was often invited to stay for one of Matilda's home-cooked Hungarian dinners.

On the menu:

— ⁂ —

Pig Knuckles
Sauerkraut

— ⁂ —

It wasn't only an appetite and polished act that developed in those basement rehearsals. When Mae West turned seventeen, she and Frank Wallace became husband and wife.

The couple never actually lived together. In fact, once she became well known, West tried to deny that the marriage ever existed, an unsuccessful ploy that backfired when both a marriage license and Mr. Wallace surfaced. The couple subsequently divorced.

Duke and Duchess of Windsor

Prince Edward became King Edward VIII upon the death of his father King George V on January 20, 1936. He was a well-traveled military veteran interested in the social problems of the day. He was a handsome and popular figure who began his reign attempting to modernize the monarchy for the twentieth century.

His reforms fell flat, however, and many royal advisors were fired, resigned or given huge salary cuts. Morale plunged. During this time, his affair with the twice-married Wallis Simpson was an open secret, protected by the press. King Edward began spending more and more time with Ms. Simpson. Finally, the king was forced to address the affair after getting a warning from his private secretary about the press' intention to publicize the affair and the threat of his government to resign en masse.

King Edward would not give up his affair with Simpson. As king and head of the Church of England, he simply could not marry his divorced lover. Just eleven months into his reign, King Edward VIII abdicated his throne, ending the shortest reign for a monarch since his namesake Edward V. Edward became the Duke of Windsor. Simpson was soon granted her second divorce, and the couple finally married. The Duke and Duchess of Windsor's union became known as perhaps the greatest love story of the twentieth century.

On December 2, 1936, King Edward VIII met with Prime Minister Baldwin to discuss the crisis caused by Edward's romance. Upon his return from that meeting, he had dinner with Wallis, her cousin Newbold Noyes and Aunt Bessie. Although not yet public, King Edward announced his decision to marry Ms. Simpson, regardless of the consequences. The consequences, of course, would be the abdication of his throne and birth of their legendary public romance.

On the menu that evening:

— —

Clear Turtle Soup
Lobster Mousse with Light Piquant Sauce
Bordeaux Wine
Roast Pheasant
Potatoes Souffle
Mixed Green Salad
Frozen Fresh Pineapple
and Toasted Cheese Savory
Coffee and Liqueurs

— —

The Duke and Duchess of Windsor were exiled to France, where apart from the Duke's brief stint as Governor of the Bahamas they lived for the rest of their lives. They were together at the Duke's death on May 28, 1972, just a month shy of his 78th birthday.

Tiger Woods

AT AGE TWO, his golf game was showcased for the first time on national television when he hit balls with Bob Hope on the Merv Griffin Show. By age three, he shot 48 for nine holes and at the ripe old age of five, he was profiled in *Golf Digest*. He had the most spectacular junior golf career in history, winning the USGA Junior World Championship three consecutive times. He entered professional golf on the heels of his unprecedented third consecutive victory in the United States Amateur, giving him six consecutive USGA championships.

With just seven tournaments available for him to try and earn a PGA card, Tiger Woods won two of them and almost $800,000 to easily qualify. In fact, *Sports Illustrated* named him 1996 Sportsman of the Year. In 1997, all he did was become the top-ranked golfer in the world and the leading money winner on the PGA Tour with victories in four tournaments.

One of those victories launched Tiger's career even farther into golfing legend: his emotional, unprecedented victory in The Masters. Tiger Woods, son of an African-American father and Thai mother, absolutely shattered almost every record at the golfing world's most beloved—and traditional—tournament. His breathtaking dominance showed the world in no uncertain terms that golf was entering a new era.

His first official duty as Masters champion was to put on the ceremonial Green jacket given to each champion signifying their membership in the exclusive club. About the only other official duty is to select the menu for the Champions Dinner held each year at the start of the following year's championship. In this duty, Tiger's 21-year-old youth certainly shined through.

On the menu:

— ❧ —

Cheeseburgers
Grilled Chicken Sandwiches
French Fries
Chocolate or Strawberry Milkshakes

— ❧ —

Tiger's dinner menu was served at the start of the 1998 Masters, which was won by Tiger's best friend and neighbor on Tour, the 46-year-old Mark O'Meara. O'Meara's menu reflected a taste more representative of the international travels their golfing life demands.

On the menu:

— ❧ —

Sushi
Steak and/or Chicken Fajitas

— ❧ —

Tiger retooled his swing in 1998, when he "slipped" all the way to fourth on the PGA Tour money list and only won three events around the world. Since then, he has dominated the golf world like no other golfer ever. His 2000-2001 Grand Slam is ranked by many as the greatest feat in golf history. He sets records and wins major tournaments almost faster than his achievements can be chronicled.

In the next *Collectible Meals*....

President Bush
September 12, 2001. The day after devastating terrorist attacks in Washington and New York, President Bush arrived back at the White House. He was met by his Chief of Staff and other senior advisors, who urged him to immediately evacuate the White House—there was a credible threat of an imminent attack.

According to Bob Woodward in the Washington Post, the President angrily, almost defiantly, rejected that advice. He then added, "And by the way, I'm hungry." He turned to Navy steward Ferdinand Garcia. "Ferdie, I want a hamburger...."

Mark Twain
Mark Twain, the great American author, toured Europe in the summer of 1878. He hated the food so much that he dreamed of the American feast he would have upon his return. He wrote about his dream, outlining the menu.....

Winston Churchill
August 15, 1942, British Prime Minister Winston Churchill was in Moscow for talks with the Russians as World War II raged. The meetings sputtered, and Churchill prepared to leave. In an attempt to salvage the talks, Russian leader Josef Stalin invited him to a meeting in Stalin's private quarters. Joined only by Molotov, the men spent all night in talks over a banquet that began with simple radishes and featured the intact head of a sucking pig....

Timothy McVeigh
Young soldier turned killer in the Oklahoma City courthouse bombing. Over 400 people died in the most vicious terrorist attack ever carried out by an American in his own country. He was captured and sentenced to die. For his last meal, he chose an all-dessert menu....

Charles Carroll
Famed Maryland patriot hosted a dinner in 1776 to send off English Governor Eden. Although he was cast out of the state for his English allegiance, he was personally liked by many in the Maryland legislature. The elaborate feast was emblematic of the awkward social times, where etiquette, politics and personal feelings posed massive contradictions....

Truman Capote and Katharine Graham
Truman Capote was one of the great authors of the 20st Century and a legendary member of the so-called "jet set." On November 28, 1966, he hosted what many called the social event of the decade, the Black and White Ball. Everyone from Frank Sinatra to Alice Roosevelt Longworth to Jerome Robbins attended. Washington Post publisher Katharine Graham was the matron of honor. Her only real obligation was to share a private meal with Capote just prior to the ball. She arranged a picnic dinner to be served in her room at the Plaza. She served "bird and a bottle...."

Venus and Serena Williams
The controversial Williams sisters are two of the most talented and exciting players on the women's professional tennis circuit. In early September, 2001, they were in New York, playing in the U.S. Open. Serena's first Grand Slam victory was at this tournament; Venus was the defending champion. The final of the 2001 event would feature the two sisters battling each other for the championship. (Venus won.) On the eve of their tournament battles, the two sisters—also doubles partners—practiced, stayed and dined together, even ordering the same menu....

Robert Tools
Robert Tools was the world's first recipient of a self-contained human heart. In July 2001, just hours from death, Louisville surgeons implanted the mechanical heart, discarding Tools' diseased one.

Although he was still very weak, Tools chose to make his first public appearance to encourage people to dine out in the aftermath of the September terrorist attacks. He was accompanied by his wife, physicians and the mayor of Louisville. Tools saved his biggest smile for the waitress, who brought him ....

Vladimir Putin
Russian President Vladimir Putin has had nuclear arms agreements at the top of his agenda through negotiations with two very different presidents, Bill Clinton and George W. Bush. On June 4, 2000, the Russian premier opened a summit meeting with President Clinton in Moscow with a "working meal" in his apartment. On the menu.... Just eighteen months later, in November of 2001, Putin was negotiating with President George W. Bush, still attempting to extend the ABM treaty which serves as the outline for the sometimes uneasy nuclear balance between the two powers. This time the meeting was in Texas, at President Bush's private residence. An old-fashioned Texas meal for thirty celebrated an agreement to shrink each nation's nuclear stockpile by two-thirds....

Pilgrims, Thanksgiving Story
Almost one full year after their arrival at Plymouth Rock, the Pilgrims celebrated a robust harvest by holding a rather traditional English festival. Grateful for the help they received in surviving their first year, they invited the Native Americans to participate in what has evolved into our Thanksgiving holiday. Roast turkey, of course, is the centerpiece of most traditional Thanksgiving meals, but it is less than clear if turkey was even served at the first festival. It is certain that pumpkin pie, the traditional Thanksgiving dessert, was not served, although a boiled pumpkin dish was available....

Judy "Black Widow" Buenoano, grandmother condemned for arsenic poisoning killing of husband, paralyzed son and attempted murder of boyfriend. Last meal....

LBJ, stunned Vice President has a quick lunch onboard Air Force One as he waits for a judge to administer the oath of office and assume the presidency from the assassinated John F. Kennedy....

Grover Cleveland, first wedding in the White House for a President; private, informal dinner in the family dining room....

George and Barbara Bush, intimate meal pre-departure of "most critical trip of Presidency" including summit to mark end of Cold War and Thanksgiving in Saudi Arabia with troops of Desert Storm....

FDR and Queen Elizabeth, 1939 White House banquet, most famous, elegant occasion in U.S. prior to World War II....

Hsing-Hsing the panda, most popular zoo attraction ever, a gift from China by Mao Tse-tung to the U.S., died at 28 after a last meal of blueberry muffin, boiled yams....

Jacqueline Kennedy, three years after the death of the President, Mrs. Kennedy was honored at a luncheon given by Mrs. Paul Mellon. The special meal was topped by a dessert served to Mrs. Kennedy by the chef himself—Renee Verdon, Mrs. Kennedy's former White House chef. The surprised—and delighted—Mrs. Kennedy hadn't seen Verdon since her days in the White House....

Roger Maris, first man to top Babe Ruth's long-standing home run record, began the historic day with his traditional breakfast from the Stage Deli in New York....

The **Herbert Hoovers** invite the **Calvin Coolidges** over for dinner prior to the stock market crash of 1929.…

Barbara Streisand and then-lover **Omar Shariff** met for special "conferences" in Shariff's hotel suite during the filming of *Funny Girl*. Room service delivered.…